Wow!
Look What
Dinosaurs
Can Do!

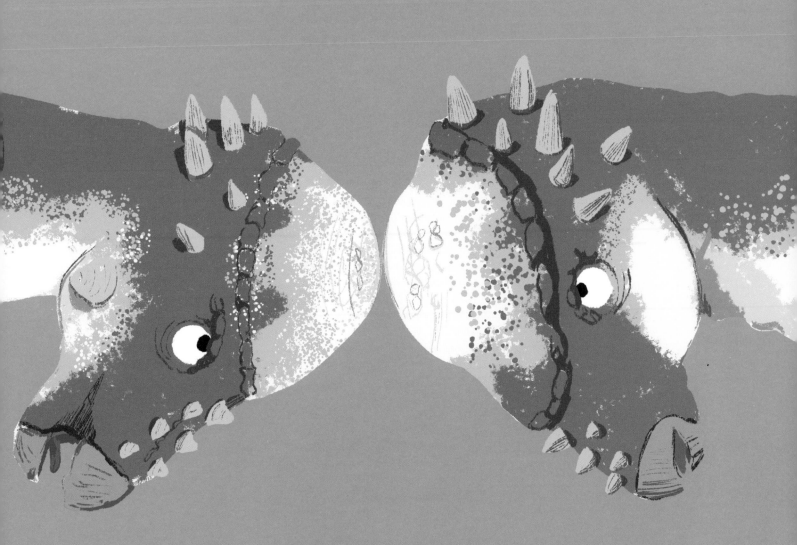

KINGFISHER
LONDON & NEW YORK

Copyright © Macmillan Publishers International Ltd 2019
Published in the United States by Kingfisher,
175 Fifth Ave., New York, NY 10010
Kingfisher is an imprint of Macmillan Children's Books, London
All right reserved.

Distributed in the U.S. and Canada by Macmillan,
175 Fifth Ave., New York, NY 10010
Library of Congress Cataloging-in-Publication data has been applied for.

Author: Jacqueline McCann
Design and styling: Liz Adcock
Cover design: Liz Adcock
Natural history consultant: Camilla de la Bédoyère
Illustrations: Ste Johnson

ISBN: 978-0-7534-7453-2 (HB)
ISBN: 978-0-7534-7454-9 (PB)

Kingfisher books are available for special promotions and premiums.
For details contact: Special Markets Department, Macmillan,
175 Fifth Ave., New York, NY 10010.

For more information, please visit
www.kingfisherbooks.com

Printed in China
9 8 7 6 5 4 3 2 1
1TR/0119/WKT/UG/140WFO

Wow!
Look What
Dinosaurs
Can Do!

KINGFISHER
LONDON & NEW YORK

Meet the dinosaurs

Hundreds of millions of years ago, incredible beasts roamed on Earth. What were they?

Dinosaurs were a kind of reptile, but they weren't anything like the crocodiles or snakes we know today. One of the first dinosaurs we know about was the fearsome meat eater Herrerasaurus.

When they first appeared, 230 million years ago, Earth was mostly a hot, dry place.

Hi, I'm **Herrerasaurus.** A goat herder in Argentina found me!

Going up . . . .

Keep going!

Guess what?

A scientist who studies dinosaurs is called a paleontologist (say pay-lee-on-toll-o-jist).

Around 200 million years ago, there was a lot more rain. Earth was a wetter place, and more plants grew.

I'm **Diplodocus**. I'm a **giant**.

Buzzzzzz off!

Diplodocus was one of the longest dinosaurs that ever lived! It was almost as long as a blue whale. How did it get so big? By eating plants!

I'm **Torosaurus**. I have horns and a beak. Impressed?

Wow!

Torosaurus had the biggest skull of any land animal—ever! It was about as big as a small car.

Fast forward to 145 million years ago, and you're in a time when Earth went through huge changes—seas flooded, the land shifted around, and there were dinosaurs everywhere!

Yikes!

5

We're hungry!

The fiercest dinosaurs were meat eaters. Their favorite snack? Other dinosaurs!

Meat-eating dinosaurs are called carnivores. They had razor-sharp teeth to tear the flesh of smaller dinosaurs, or to eat dead ones.

One of the most famous dinosaurs ever discovered is the giant T. rex. It was as tall as a giraffe and bigger than two elephants!

I'm Tyrannosaurus rex. You can call me Mr T. rex.

I'm compsognathus. (say comp-sog-nay-thus)

Compsognathus was a dainty little dino. It was the size of a turkey, and its favorite meal was lizard. Slurrrp!

Wow!
Dragonflies, spiders, and many other creepy-crawlies have been around for 300 million years.

Move over, T. rex, I'm Giganotosaurus.

Not so fast!

Feeling feathery

Yutyrannus huali lived in China and came from the same family as T. rex. Scientists discovered it was covered in long, wispy feathers!

If you thought T. rex was big, think again! Scientists in Argentina, in South America, discovered an even bigger carnivore, which they called "giant southern lizard," or Giganotosaurus.

7

A spiny giant

Meet Spinosaurus, or "spine lizard." It's the biggest meat-eating dinosaur ever discovered!

With jaws like a crocodile, a long, scaly neck, and a huge body with a strange fin on its back, Spinosaurus was the biggest, strangest, deadliest carnivore ever!

Most meat-eating dinosaurs lived on land, but not Spinosaurus. It liked to swim in rivers and salty water around North Africa.

I'm Spinosaurus.

Spinosaurus came from a family of fish-eating dinosaurs. They all had sharp, cone-shaped teeth and huge curved claws—perfect for catching and eating slippery fish, squid, and even sharks.

Spine tingling

No one knows for sure why Spinosaurus had an enormous sail-like fin on its back. Maybe the fin changed color and helped the Spinosaurus attract a new mate?

Like crocodiles today, the nostrils on Spinosaurus were on the top of its snout. It lay with its body under the water, waiting to pounce, but was still able to breathe.

I need fishy treats . . . NOW!

Wow!

Mawsonia was a huge fish that swam in ancient seas and was hunted by Spinosaurus. Its relative, the coelacanth (say seal-a-canth), still swims in the Indian Ocean today.

Spinosaurus prowled on land, too, on two massive hind legs!

I'm a coelacanth. You can't catch me!

I'm Mawsonia—watch out!

Powerful packs

How did little carnivores hunt? They got together and hunted in packs—and they were ferocious!

About 110 million years ago, a big, plant-eating dinosaur, called Tenontosaurus, and a much smaller meat eater, called Deinonychus, lived in the same place, where North America is today.

I'm Tenontosaurus. Take that! Thwack!

Hunting in a pack was the best way for Deinonychus (say die-non-e-cus) to overpower and bring down a large dinosaur.

Hey, it's dinnertime!

Wow!

Paleontologists believe that Deinonychus had feathers, like its little cousin Velociraptor.

Deinonychus wasn't big, but it was nimble and used its powerful legs to pounce. Then it went to work with its strong jaws.

My name means "terrible claw."

who goes there?

OW! Get off!

Deinonychus had an incredibly powerful bite. Once it locked its teeth into something, it was almost impossible to escape.

11

Mighty plant lovers

The giants of the dinosaur world were the tree-topping plant eaters, called sauropods.

For more than 150 million years, the sauropods (say sawr-o-pods) roamed on Earth. They are some of the biggest creatures that have ever lived. They are called herbivores (plant eaters), because they ate plants.

I'm Mamenchisaurus.

Wow!

On a small island off Scotland, scientists have discovered huge sauropod footprints on the rocky shore. The footprints are so big that no one noticed them before!

The sauropods had a lot in common besides being giants. They all had a tiny head, a super-long neck and tail, a huge body, and legs like tree trunks!

Tail alert!

Any meat-eater that tried to take a bite out of Mamenchisaurus got a mighty thwack!

I'm Apatosaurus.
Don't mess with me.

Wow!

Scientists have discovered sauropod bones buried all over Earth—even in icy Antarctica!

The hefty Apatosaurus may have had another trick for scaring away carnivores. It could probably stand on its back legs and tower over anything that tried to take a bite.

G'day! I'm Diamantinasaurus.

Flowers! For me?

Fossils from a young Diamantinasaurus sauropod were found in Australia. Perhaps it was attracted to the plants around a stinky swamp—and got stuck in the mud—or was killed by another dino.

DDDDreadnoughtus

Do you want to meet the biggest creature ever to walk on planet Earth? Go ahead . . . it's safe.

Dreadnoughtus (say dred-nawt-us) had a suuuuper-long neck, and a suuuuper-long tail to counter-balance at the other end.

These pretty flowers appeared about **100** million years ago!

I am Dreadnoughtus, and I fear nothing!

Top to tail

Dreadnoughtus measured 85 feet (26 meters) from end to end. That's even longer than two school buses. And it weighed about 66 tons, the same as 15 elephants!

The bones in Dreadnoughtus's neck contained many tiny air holes. These helped keep the dino's neck lightweight (and possibly cooled it down, too), so Dreadnoughtus could lift its head and munch on leaves high up.

When you're this big, you don't need to move far . . . or fast! But you do need to eat a lot. Once Dreadnoughtus had munched a huge patch of forest, all it had to do was take a few steps and start clearing another patch.

Wow!

Scientists may have discovered an even bigger dino! Patagotitan was found in Argentina and may have been as heavy as a space shuttle!

Ancient spider alert!

We stick together

With all those scary carnivores on the prowl, the little plant eaters stuck together for safety!

For many dinosaurs, the safest place to be was in a herd. Together they could take care of their babies and find new grazing grounds.

Herd of Triceratops coming through!

scuttle, scuttle.

We're Struthiomimus, and we're built for speed!

Look quickly and you might think this dinosaur is an ancient ostrich. But although Struthiomimus was covered in fine feathers and sprinted on strong legs, it had two short feathered arms as well.

Tasty!

Struthiomimus had a toothless beak and long claws. Scientists think that as well as eating plants, this dino probably ate insects, too.

Eat up!

Stegosaurus, the best-known stegosaur, had a tiny head and a horned beak. It ate a huge amount and grew 30 feet (9 meters) long—as big as a truck!

Here's a strange-looking dinosaur! Tuojiangosaurus (say toh-hwang-o-sawr-us) was named after the Tuo River in China. It belonged to a famous dinosaur family called the stegosaurs.

We're Tuojiangosauruses. Have you seen any plants?

Triceratops was a plant-eating dinosaur that looked a little like a frilled rhino. It roamed in large herds, looking for fresh grazing grounds—just like buffalo do today!

Footprints! Who's there?

Hi, Stegosaurus!

The biggest and most famous of all the stegosaurs was . . . Stegosaurus.

With huge, spiky plates along its back, and a tiny head, Stegosaurus was odd looking, even 150 million years ago. It lived on plants but grew to be nearly 30 feet (9 meters) from head to tail!

We're **Stegosauruses**. Don't call us pinheads.

One smack from Stegosaurus's spiky tail would have smashed a carnivore's leg. Or made a hole. Ouch!

Feet first

Stegosaurus had five toes on its front feet and three toes on its back feet!

Left, right, Left, right.

Scientists aren't sure why Stegosaurus had such huge, bony back plates. Did they soak up the sun's rays and keep the dinosaur warm? Did they protect against meat eaters? Or did stegosaurs recognize each other by their plates?

I have a Lot of plates!

Brainy?
Stegosaurus had a brain the size of a dog's, but its body was at least 100 times bigger! Scientists think it probably wasn't very smart.

swooop! what's that?

Stegosaurus chewed tough plants that grew close to the ground. Like many other plant eaters, it had a tough, horny beak for chomping leaves, and 150 small leaf-shaped teeth for munching.

one of my plates is almost as big as you!

19

Deadly weapons

Which dino had the scariest spikes, or the most terrifying teeth? Let's find out.

I'm Pterodaustro. I have **1,000 teeth!**

I'm Carnotaurus. My name means "**meat bull.**"

Pterodaustro (say ter-o-dow-stro) was a huge flying reptile. It had a very long bill with sharp, pointy teeth, which were perfect for catching fish.

Whiplash!

The mighty sauropods, like Diplodocus, didn't have claws or spikes, but their massive tail could swoop around so fast that it could send any meat eater flying!

Triceratops, which means "three-horned face," was a beast! When it lowered its enormous horns, it could puncture a hole in T. rex's leg!

No time to chat, I've got Lunch to catch!

One of the scariest carnivores was Carnotaurus. With bull-like horns on the top of its head and powerful jaws with huge teeth, most herbivores didn't stand a chance against it.

Baryonyx was a meat-eating dinosaur that also liked fish. It had mighty hooked claws on each arm—perfect for grasping slippery scales.

Baryonyx

T. rex, the king of the dinosaurs, also had a king-size bite! It had 60 razor-sharp teeth and had the strongest bite of any land animal . . . ever!

T. rex

Therizinosaurus

Therizinosaurus (say ther-i-zeen-o-sawr-us) means "scythe lizard." This dino had claws around 3 feet (1 meter) in length.

scratchy, scratch!

21

Cool armor

Dinosaur days were dangerous times, but plant eaters had cool ways to defend themselves.

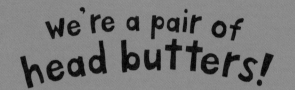

We're a pair of **head butters!**

Pachycephalosaurus (say pak-ee-sef-a-loh-sawr-us) had a very strange head. It had a very thick skull, which it probably used to have head-bashing competitions, kind of like rams do today.

Wow!

Pachycephalosaurus means "thick-headed lizard," and it was a record breaker in skull terms. The solid bone at the top of its head was about the size of a soccer ball!

Thumbs up!

Iguanadon was a plant lover with a huge thumb spike. The spike was perfect for jabbing any meat eaters that came sniffing around.

I'm AnkyLoSauruS. Back off!

ouch!

Ankylosaurus wasn't a big dinosaur, but it was still the size of a massive bull. It had tough, bony armor on its head and body, and its special weapon was a huge bone at the end of its tail!

Kentrosaurus was a stegosaur with enormous spikes along its back and tail—each one was the size of a baseball bat! It was almost impossible to attack this dinosaur.

23

Beasts of the deep

While dinosaurs ruled the land, enormous reptiles swam in the ocean. Take a deep breath . . .

These underwater reptiles were super swimmers, but they had to come to the surface to breathe, just like today's whales and dolphins.

I'm ophthalmosaurus.

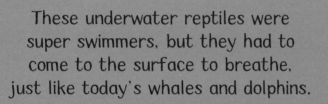

Ophthalmosaurus (say off-thal-mo-sawr-us) had a long, pointy jaw that was perfect for snapping up squid and fast-moving fish.

Eye spy

Ophthalmosaurus had eyes as big as soccer balls, which helped it see in the deep, dark ocean. Its name means "eye lizard."

One of the deadliest hunters ever to swim in the ocean was Pliosaurus. Its head was twice the size of a T. rex, and its teeth were as long as a 12-inch (30-centimeter) school ruler!

I'm Pliosaurus. Bye-bye turtle

Hi, I am **ELASMOSAURUS.**

What's that buzzing?

What a neck!

Elasmosaurus (say elaz-mo-sawr-us) had such a long neck that it could sneak up on fish and other ocean creatures without them noticing!

I am **MOSASAURUS. Open wide!**

Swim for it!

Mosasaurus (say moss-a-sawr-us) was an underwater giant! It had smooth, snake-like skin, which made it streamlined, FAST, and almost impossible to escape from!

25

High in the sky

During the time of the dinosaurs, the sky was filled with strange flying reptiles called pterosaurs.

i'm Quetzalcoatlus—come fly with me.

i'm Pteranodon. i'm toothless.

Pteranodon means "toothless wing." This huge flying reptile soared in the skies above the oceans in search of its favorite foods—fish and squid

SNAP!

buzzz buzzz

buzzz

Quetzalcoatlus (say ket-sal-coat-lus) was the largest flying creature ever! It was as tall as a giraffe, and its wings were as wide as a small plane.

The first creatures to fly were insects. They took to the skies about 400 million years ago

i'm Dimorphodon.

This scary-looking pterosaur had an enormous head. It could fly, but it also scampered up trees, gripping with its strong claws.

smile!

i'm Dsungaripterus.

Can you say zung-are-ipt-er-us? This pterosaur, with its odd-shaped beak, flew by the ocean where China is today.

Dinner

Pterosaurs loved to eat lizards, frogs, and insects. Big pterosaurs probably ate Beelzebufo, which was about the size of a beach ball.

burp!

i'm Ichthyornis.
(say ick-thee-or-nis)

Look out, i'm a bird with teeth!

Mighty explosion

About 65 million years ago, almost all living things on Earth died suddenly. What happened?

Scientists think a massive rock from outer space, called an asteroid, crashed into Earth. It left an enormous crater in the ground, which can still be seen today in Mexico.

BOOOOM!

LOOK OUT!

Hot and cold

When the asteroid crashed, it sent up huge clouds of hot dust that stayed in the air for a long time. The ash blocked out the sunlight, Earth grew colder, and plants died.

When the asteroid hit, it made volcanoes all over the world erupt! Poisonous gases and ash clouds poured out for thousands of years. It was almost impossible for any creature to survive.

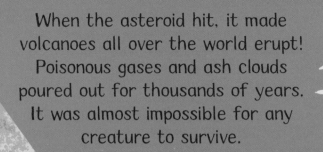

Wow!

Scientists think that roughly 90 percent of all living creatures died 65 million years ago. It was a catastrophe!

After the dust had settled, the only dinosaurs left alive were the ones we call "birds." Other animals that also survived the asteroid crash eventually became the huge range of creatures alive on Earth today.

It was a total wipeout.

Feathered friends

It's hard to believe, but all the birds you see today are descended from the dinosaurs.

Long before the asteroid hit Earth, some dinosaurs had started to have bird-like features—for example, a small body, feathers, and no teeth.

I'm Deinonychus. Maybe I looked like this?

No one knows what color the first feathers were, but brown, gray, black, and chestnut-brown are the most likely colors.

In China

Scientists have found many amazing dinosaur remains in China. Many of the remains have feathers!

My great-great-great (x 1 million) grandfather was . . . **T. rex!**

I wonder if he had feathers, too?

Wow!

There are more than 10,000 kinds of birds on Earth today—and they all came from dinosaurs.

I'm **Archaeopteryx,** and I'm the first bird!

I'm **confuciusornis,** and I can fly!

Scientists think the first bird lived 150 million years ago. It's called Archaeopteryx (say ark-ee-op-ter-ix), and it had sharp teeth in its beak!

Confuciusornis (say con-few-shuss-or-nis) was about the size of a crow. It had wings, long tail feathers, and a toothless beak—just like birds today!

31

How do we know?

The dinosaurs lived millions of years ago. When they died, they left traces of themselves behind—in rock!

When a dinosaur died, its body was sometimes trapped in layers of mud and ash. Over millions of years, the layers and the bones turned to stone and created a fossil.

WOW, a stegosaur fossil!

can you see its back plates?

Scientists have discovered that ancient dinosaur poop turned into fossils, too!

Scientists can even tell what dinos had for lunch. The massive sauropods ate stones, to grind down the plants in their belly!

Mmmm stones. Yum!

Wow!

In 1811, an English paleontologist named Mary Anning discovered the first ichthyosaur fossil. People thought it was a strange crocodile, but they soon realized it was a prehistoric ocean reptile!